EP Second Reader
Workbook

I'm _____.

This is my workbook. My favorite books are

_____

_____

_____

The vocabulary in this workbook is based on, and
used by permission of, Easy Peasy All-in-One Homeschool.
For EP's online curriculum visit www.allinonehomeschool.com

ISBN-13: 978-1505417692
ISBN-10: 1505417694

About This Workbook

This is an offline workbook of vocabulary puzzles and games for Easy Peasy All-in-One Homeschool's reading course for Level 2. We've modified and expanded upon the online activities available at the Easy Peasy All-in-One Homeschool website (www.allinonehomeschool.com) so that your child can work offline if desired. Whether you use the online or offline versions, or a combination of both, your child will enjoy these supplements to the Easy Peasy reading course.

How to Use This Workbook

This workbook is designed to be used as a complement to Easy Peasy's reading curriculum, either the online or offline version. It provides ample activities to help your child master the vocabulary words in Level 2. For any given lesson, use the Activity List to pick out an activity and have your child work on it. Here's our suggestion:

Use the worksheets with lesson numbers for the specified lessons when:
- New vocabulary words are first introduced.
- The online course or EP reader instructs to review the vocabulary words or to play an online vocabulary game.

Use the additional worksheets any time during the course when:
- Your child needs more practice on a specific vocabulary set.
- Your child wants extra activities just for fun.

If your child initially has difficulty remembering all the words, don't worry. The first activity for each vocabulary set is to review all the words and their meanings. The matching activities provided are another a great way to reinforce the meanings of the words in preparation for the more challenging exercises in the workbook.

The solutions to selected activities are included at the end of the workbook.

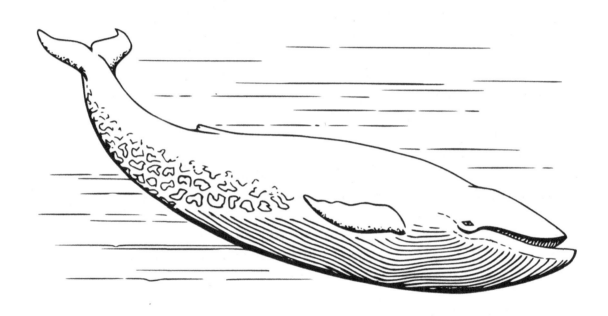

Activity List

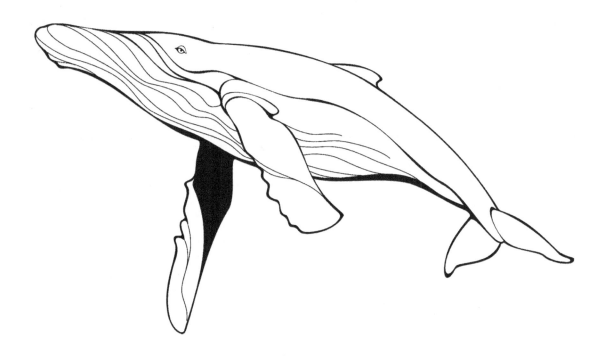

Lily's Walk Vocabulary

Review and read aloud the words and their meanings.

slumber = sleep

contented = happy and at ease

gleam = shine brightly

bulge = swelling or protruding

wallow = lie relaxed in mud or water

demolish = knock down a building

tirelessly = with endless energy, working without getting tired

emulate = imitate someone to try to achieve what they have

intently = with great focus, with eager attention

exasperated = frustrated, very irritated

disrepair = poor condition of a building because no one is caring for it

✓ The moonlight <u>gleamed</u> on the water.
✓ Her pockets were <u>bulging</u> with presents.
✓ She <u>intently</u> looked into my eyes.
✓ She fell into a deep and peaceful <u>slumber</u>.
✓ I was <u>exasperated</u> by his endless grumbling.
✓ The factory is due to be <u>demolished</u> next year.
✓ Classical music made them <u>contented</u> and restful.
✓ The building has fallen into <u>disrepair</u> over the years.
✓ The boy tried to <u>emulate</u> the famous baseball player.
✓ We work <u>tirelessly</u> to ensure the streets are safe and clean.
✓ Pigs do not sweat, so they <u>wallow</u> in mud to cool their bodies.

Lily's Walk Matching

Can you match the words with their definitions?

disrepair   **SLUMBER**   *tirelessly*   demolish   gleam   WaLLoW

emulate   *intently*   **BULGE**   contented   **exasperated**

_____ = with great focus, with eager attention

_____ = lie relaxed in mud or water

_____ = knock down a building

_____ = frustrated, very irritated

_____ = swelling or protruding

_____ = happy and at ease

_____ = shine brightly

_____ = sleep

_____ = with endless energy, working without getting tired

_____ = poor condition of a building because no one is caring for it

_____ = imitate someone to try to achieve what they have

Lily's Walk Word Search

Find the hidden words and explain their meanings. The words can go in any direction, even backwards! (The solution is on page 72.)

G	E	W	F	V	L	W	R	I	D
D	R	T	P	J	O	N	N	R	E
N	I	U	A	L	L	T	P	E	T
A	M	S	L	L	E	G	D	B	A
J	V	A	R	N	U	X	L	M	R
C	W	N	T	E	L	M	Q	U	E
O	X	L	J	H	P	U	E	L	P
N	Y	O	F	D	M	A	R	S	S
T	B	U	L	G	E	V	I	Y	A
E	S	W	G	Y	K	I	O	R	X
N	H	S	I	L	O	M	E	D	E
T	I	R	E	L	E	S	S	L	Y
E	C	I	E	S	Z	A	W	H	B
D	M	K	T	D	M	W	M	Z	P
Q	E	W	B	Q	H	T	Q	K	C

bulge

gleam

wallow

slumber

emulate

intently

demolish

disrepair

tirelessly

contented

exasperated

Lily's Walk Crossword

Across

6. with great focus, with eager attention
7. happy and at ease
8. shine brightly
9. frustrated, very irritated
10. with endless energy, working without getting tired

Down

1. swelling or protruding
2. imitate someone to try to achieve what they have
3. sleep
4. lie relaxed in mud or water
5. poor condition of a building because no one is caring for it

Lily's Walk Multiple Choice

Choose the word from the definition or the definition from the word.

 with great focus, with eager attention

○ wallow   ○ intently   ○ contented   ○ tirelessly

 poor condition of a building because no one is caring for it

○ disrepair   ○ demolish   ○ slumber   ○ exasperated

 imitate someone to try to achieve what they have

○ gleam   ○ bulge   ○ emulate   ○ wallow

 exasperated

○ lie relaxed in mud or water

○ frustrated, very irritated

○ with endless energy

○ with great focus

 demolish

○ swelling or protruding

○ happy and at ease

○ shine brightly

○ knock down a building

 slumber

○ sleep

○ poor condition of a building

○ frustrated, very irritated

○ working without getting tired

 wallow

○ lie relaxed in mud or water

○ frustrated, very irritated

○ shine brightly

○ sleep

Old Mr. Toad Vocabulary

Review and read aloud the words and their meanings.

> anxious = worried
>
> envy = jealous
>
> hastily = doing something in a hurry
>
> feeble = lacking physical strength
>
> indignant = feeling angered or annoyed
>
> amble = walking in a slow, relaxed way
>
> smug = having too much pride in yourself
>
> scorn = thinking that someone or something is worthless or despicable

Peter Rabbit finds
Old Mr. Toad

✓ Her grandfather is too <u>feeble</u> to work.
✓ The rich man was <u>smug</u> and unfriendly.
✓ She <u>scorned</u> their views as old-fashioned.
✓ Parents are naturally <u>anxious</u> for their children.
✓ I <u>hastily</u> finished my homework before the game started.
✓ She was full of <u>envy</u> when her sister won the contest.
✓ He was very <u>indignant</u> at the way he had been treated.
✓ We like to <u>amble</u> through the park on Saturdays.

Old Mr. Toad Matching

Can you match the words with their definitions?

hastily	o	o	worried
anxious	o	o	jealous
indignant	o	o	doing something in a hurry
envy	o	o	lacking physical strength
scorn	o	o	feeling angered or annoyed
feeble	o	o	walking in a slow, relaxed way
amble	o	o	having too much pride in yourself
smug	o	o	thinking that someone or something is worthless or despicable

Old Mr. Toad Spelling

Can you spell all the words?

jealous

E		V	

worried

	N	X			U	S

walking in a slow, relaxed way

A	M			E

having too much pride in yourself

	M		G

thinking that someone or something is worthless or despicable

S	C		R	

feeling angered or annoyed

I	N			G		N	T

doing something in a hurry

H		S		I		Y

lacking physical strength

F		E		L	E

Jimmy Skunk Vocabulary

Review and read aloud the words and their meanings.

shrewd = clever

injustice = unfair

dignity = having honor and respect

thoughtless = selfish, thinking only of yourself

acquaintance = someone you know, but not really well

impudent = not showing respect to someone who deserves respect

admire = to have a good opinion of something, to respect someone

suspicion = a feeling or belief that someone is guilty or that a certain thought is true

✓ The boy who cheated won the game. What an <u>injustice</u>!
✓ He was arrested on <u>suspicion</u> of being a spy.
✓ She accepted the criticism with quiet <u>dignity</u>.
✓ His <u>thoughtless</u> remark made them angry.
✓ He is not a friend, only an <u>acquaintance</u>.
✓ The <u>shrewd</u> man devised a secret plan.
✓ How could you be so <u>impudent</u>?
✓ I really <u>admire</u> your enthusiasm.

Jimmy Skunk visits
Jonny Chuck's Old House

Jimmy Skunk Matching

Connect each word with its definition.

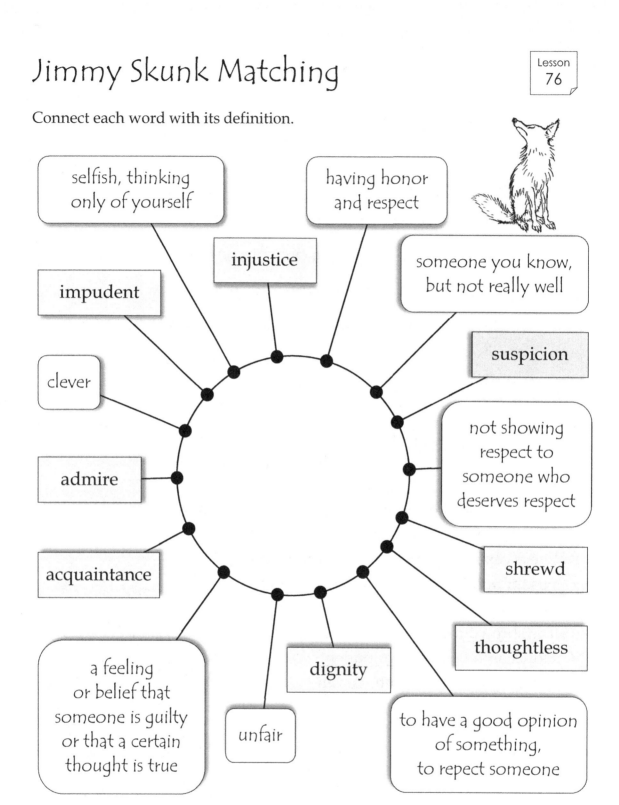

selfish, thinking
only of yourself

having honor
and respect

injustice

impudent

someone you know,
but not really well

clever

suspicion

admire

not showing
respect to
someone who
deserves respect

acquaintance

shrewd

thoughtless

a feeling
or belief that
someone is guilty
or that a certain
thought is true

dignity

unfair

to have a good opinion
of something,
to repect someone

Jimmy Skunk Word Jumble

Unscramble the jumbled words.

 having honor and respect

I D I T Y N G _____

 not showing respect to someone who deserves respect

T I N P E D U M _____

 someone you know, but not really well

A Q N C T A A U N I E C _____

 to have a good opinion of something, to respect someone

E A R D M I _____

 unfair

I I N C E S J T U _____

 selfish, thinking only of yourself

H T E L U H T S O G S _____

 clever

D H R W S E _____

 a feeling or belief that someone is guilty

P S U S I I O N C _____

Vocabulary Review Matching I

Can you match the words with their definitions?

contented   **disrepair**   envy   intently   SHreWd   indignant

feeble   **injustice**   dignity   **anxious**   gleam   **aMBLe**

_____ = having honor and respect

_____ = walking in a slow, relaxed way

_____ = with great focus, with eager attention

_____ = happy and at ease

_____ = angry and annoyed

_____ = shine brightly

_____ = worried

_____ = unfair

_____ = weak

_____ = clever

_____ = jealous

_____ = poor condition of a building
because no one is caring for it

Vocabulary Review Matching II

Can you match the words with their definitions?

tirelessly	sleep
demolish	jealous
slumber	with endless energy
bulge	swelling or protruding
wallow	knock down a building
envy	having honor and respect
emulate	frustrated, very irritated
smug	selfish, thinking only of yourself
hastily	doing something in a hurry
dignity	lie relaxed in mud or water
disrepair	having too much pride in yourself
thoughtless	poor condition of a building because no one is caring for it
exasperated	imitate someone to try to achieve what they have

Vocabulary Review Matching III

Can you match the words with their definitions?

impudent   *thoughtless*   dignity   acquaintance

scorn   Indignant   **SUSPICION**   Feeble   admire

_____ = lacking physical strength

_____ = feeling angered or annoyed

_____ = having honor and respect

_____ = selfish, thinking only of yourself

_____ = someone you know, but not really well

_____ = not showing respect to someone who deserves respect

_____ = to have a good opinion of something, to respect someone

_____ = thinking that someone or something is worthless or despicable

_____ = a feeling or belief that someone is guilty or that a certain thought is true

Vocabulary Review Multiple Choice I

Choose the word from the definition or the definition from the word.

 worried

O amble   O demolish   O anxious   O envy

 shine brightly

O gleam   O wallow   O scorn   O suspicion

 emulate

O having honor and respect

O having too much pride in yourself

O imitate someone to try to achieve what they have

 feeble

O lacking physical strength

O someone you know, but not really well

O a feeling or belief that someone is guilty

 admire

O to respect someone

O jealous

O thinking only of yourself

O swelling or protruding

 injustice

O frustrated, very irritated

O knock down a building

O unfair

O sleep

Vocabulary Review Multiple Choice II

Choose the word from the definition or the definition from the word.

 jealous

○ dignity ○ injustice ○ suspicion ○ envy

 with endless energy, working without getting tired

○ bulge ○ tirelessly ○ indignant ○ thoughtless

 hastily

○ feeling angered or annoyed

○ imitate someone to try to achieve what they have

○ doing something in a hurry

 exasperated

○ frustrated, very irritated

○ doing something in a hurry

○ not showing respect to someone who deserves respect

 shrewd

○ clever

○ thinking only of yourself

○ to respect someone

○ with great focus

 demolish

○ having respect

○ lie relaxed in mud

○ knock down a building

○ lie relaxed in mud or water

Vocabulary Review Multiple Choice III

Choose the word from the definition or the definition from the word.

 unfair

○ dignity   ○ injustice   ○ suspicion   ○ thoughtless

frustrated, very irritated

○ feeble   ○ intently   ○ impudent   ○ exasperated

scorn

○ imitate someone to try to achieve what they have

○ to have a good opinion of something, to respect someone

○ thinking that someone or something is worthless or despicable

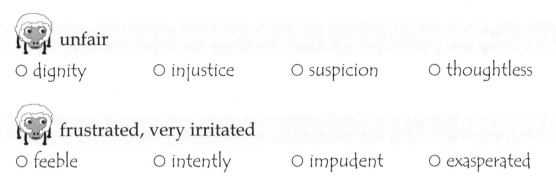

acquaintance

○ knock down a building

○ someone you know, but not really well

○ selfish, thinking only of yourself

bulge

○ in a hurry

○ jealous

○ protruding

smug

○ having too much pride in yourself

○ feeling angered or annoyed

○ walking in a slow, relaxed way

○ doing something in a hurry

contented

○ sleep

○ clever

○ happy and at ease

○ worried

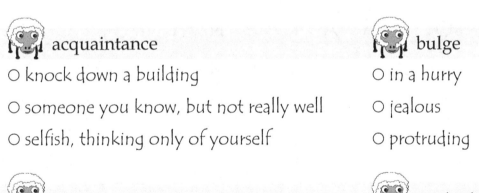
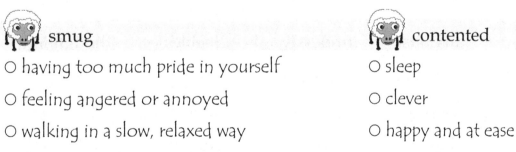

Vocabulary Review Word Search

Find the hidden words and explain their meanings. The words can go in any direction, even backwards! (The solution is on page 72.)

```
T  D  S  F  E  E  B  L  E  D  G  J  B  D
N  E  S  D  M  I  H  E  A  R  L  U  E  I
A  M  E  C  S  I  N  Y  D  X  E  T  L  S
N  O  L  I  U  B  N  J  Z  B  A  I  G  R
G  L  T  P  O  W  U  T  U  R  M  K  E  E
I  I  H  T  I  R  E  L  E  S  S  L  Y  P
D  S  G  J  X  E  V  P  G  N  T  Q  B  A
N  H  U  Q  N  Y  S  R  D  E  T  I  J  I
I  E  O  F  A  A  K  C  N  H  F  L  C  R
K  A  H  Q  X  Y  T  I  N  G  I  D  Y  E
C  Z  T  E  Z  D  E  T  N  E  T  N  O  C
Y  V  N  E  G  I  M  P  U  D  E  N  T  A
```

anxious	tirelessly	feeble	thoughtless
demolish	injustice	intently	contented
dignity	gleam	impudent	disrepair
bulge	envy	exasperated	indignant

Lily's Walk Matching

Can you match the words with their definitions?

bulge

poor condition of a building because no one is caring for it

slumber

happy and at ease

demolish

sleep

wallow

with great focus

contented

swelling or protruding

disrepair

lie relaxed in mud or water

emulate

knock down a building

intently

frustrated, very irritated

gleam

with endless energy

exasperated

shine brightly

tirelessly

imitate someone to try to achieve what they have

Lily's Walk Spelling

swelling or protruding

B		L		E	

shine brightly

G	L			M

sleep

S		U		B		R	

happy and at ease

C		N					E	D

with endless energy, working without getting tired

T	I			L		S			Y

frustrated, very irritated

E	X			P		R		T	E	

poor condition of a building because no one is caring for it

D			R	E			I		

imitate someone to try to achieve what they have

E	M			A		

Lily's Walk Word Jumble

Unscramble the jumbled words.

sleep

MEBSRLU → _____

happy and at ease

NOTCTNEDE → _____

shine brightly

ALMEG → _____

swelling or protruding

EUBLG → _____

with endless energy, working without getting tired

LRSSYEIELT → _____

poor condition of a building because no one is caring for it

REISADRPI → _____

with great focus, with eager attention

TIENNTYL → _____

frustrated, very irritated

PXEATEERSDA → _____

Lily's Walk Fill-in-the-Blanks

Fill in the blanks to complete the sentences. Change the word forms if necessary.

emulate   bulge   SLUMBER   wallow   disrepair   gleam

tirelessly   CONTENTED   intently   demolish   exasperated

1. The moonlight _____ on the water.

2. I was _____ by his endless grumbling.

3. Her pockets were _____ with presents.

4. She fell into a deep and peaceful _____.

5. She _____ looked into my eyes.

6. The factory is due to be _____ next year.

7. Classical music made them _____ and restful.

8. The building has fallen into _____ over the years.

9. The boy tried to _____ the famous baseball player.

10. We work _____ to ensure the streets are safe and clean.

11. Pigs do not sweat, so they _____ in mud to cool their bodies.

Old Mr. Toad Crossword

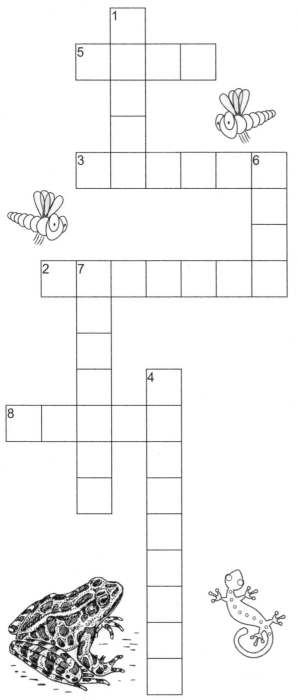

Across

2. doing something in a hurry
3. lacking physical strength
5. having too much pride in yourself
8. thinking that someone or something is worthless or despicable

Down

1. walking in a slow, relaxed way
4. feeling angered or annoyed
6. jealous
7. worried

Here's what Mr. Toad says;
Heed it well, my dear:
"Time to watch for clouds is
When the sky is clear."
- *The Adventures of Old Mr. Toad*

Old Mr. Toad Word Jumble

Unscramble the jumbled words.

walking in a slow, relaxed way

LAMBE → _____

worried

OAISUNX → _____

jealous

NYVE → _____

lacking physical strength

EBEEFL → _____

doing something in a hurry

YLAHTIS → _____

feeling angered or annoyed

DANINGITN → _____

Having too much pride in your self

UMGS → _____

thinking that someone or something or worthless or despicable

SONCR → _____

Old Mr. Toad Word Search

Find the hidden words and explain their meanings. The words can go in any direction, even backwards! (The solution is on page 72.)

E	U	S	Q	B	S	D	G	U	I	G	X	C	A
N	L	K	M	M	J	A	Y	B	N	T	N	O	W
I	A	B	X	U	N	X	E	X	D	E	R	I	F
F	S	G	E	X	G	L	F	H	I	Y	O	R	M
R	C	Q	I	E	B	P	D	Z	G	T	C	K	B
A	V	O	H	M	F	H	B	F	N	E	S	D	Q
O	U	T	A	N	K	V	A	U	A	U	I	F	J
S	V	Y	L	I	T	S	A	H	N	O	B	V	G
L	F	W	J	R	D	S	E	P	T	Y	N	S	A
E	N	V	Y	H	X	L	A	I	V	G	W	C	Z

amble   feeble   scorn   anxious

hastily   envy   smug   indignant

Old Mother Nature doth provide
For all her children, large or small.
Her wisdom foresees all their needs
And makes provision for them all.
- *The Adventures of Old Mr. Toad*

Old Mr. Toad Word Pieces

Use the pieces below to build words with the given definitions.

worried

| IO | X | US | AN | → | _____ |

feeling angered or annoyed

| IGN | ANT | IND | → | _____ |

doing something in a hurry

| ILY | HAS | T | → | _____ |

thinking that someone or something is worthless or despicable

| CO | S | RN | → | _____ |

having too much pride in yourself

| G | U | SM | → | _____ |

jealous

| E | Y | NV | → | _____ |

lacking physical strength

| B | FEE | LE | → | _____ |

Old Mr. Toad Fill-in-the-Blanks

Fill in the blanks to complete the sentences. Change the word forms if necessary.

anxious	feeble	ENVY	indignant
smug	Scorn	amble	hastily

1. Her grandfather is too _____ to work.

2. She _____ their views as old-fashioned.

3. Parents are naturally _____ for their children.

4. He was very _____ at the way he had been treated.

5. She was full of _____ when her sister won the contest.

6. I _____ finished my homework before the game started.

7. We like to _____ through the park on Saturdays.

8. The rich man was _____ and unfriendly.

"Beetle, Beetle, smooth and smug,
You are nothing but a bug.
Bugs are made for Skunks to eat,
So come out from your retreat."
- *The Adventures of Old Mr. Toad*

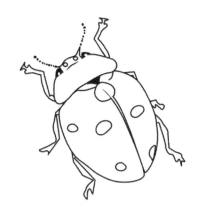

Jimmy Skunk Spelling

not showing respect to someone who deserves respect

I	M			D			

to respect someone

	D	M			

clever

S				W	

Jimmy Skunk talks to Sammy Jay

unfair

I	N					C	

a feeling or belief that someone is guilty

S			P				N

selfish, thinking only of yourself

T					H	T				

someone you know, but not really well

	C	Q				T			C	

Jimmy Skunk Crossword

Across
6. clever
8. selfish, thinking only of yourself

Down
1. unfair
2. someone you know, but not really well
3. not showing respect to someone who deserves respect
4. to have a good opinion of something, to respect someone
5. having honor and respect
7. a feeling or belief that someone is guilty or that a certain thought is true

Jimmy Skunk Word Search

Find the hidden words and explain their meanings. (The solution is on page 72.)

thoughtless   impudent   INJUSTICE   dignity   admire

SHreWd   suspicion   acquaintance   scold

Jimmy Skunk Fill-in-the-Blanks

Fill in the blanks to complete the sentences. Change the word forms if necessary.

thoughtless   impudent   INJUSTICE   dignity

admire   SHreWd   suspicion   acquaintance

1. The boy who cheated won the game. What an _____!

2. He was arrested on _____ of being a spy.

3. She accepted the criticism with quiet _____.

4. His _____ remark made them angry.

5. The _____ man devised a secret plan.

6. He is not a friend, only an _____.

7. How could you be so _____?

8. I really _____
   your enthusiasm.

Jimmy Skunk bumps
into Unc' Billy.

Jimmy Skunk Multiple Choice

Choose the word from the definition or the definition from the word.

 selfish, thinking only of yourself

O dignity   O injustice   O shrewd   O thoughtless

 acquaintance

O having honor and respect

O someone you know, but not really well

O not showing respect to someone who deserves respect

O a feeling or belief that someone is guilty

 suspicion

O knock down a building

O frustrated, very irritated

O a feeling or belief that someone is guilty

O not showing respect to someone who deserves respect

 dignity

O jealous

O having honor and respect

O walking in a slow, relaxed way

O having too much pride in yourself

Vocabulary Review Word Search

Find the hidden words and explain their meanings. The words can go in any direction, even backwards! (The solution is on page 73.)

A	E	T	K	C	B	A	S	T	I
S	D	L	O	H	F	C	H	G	E
J	X	M	B	M	H	Q	R	U	T
H	Y	U	I	M	R	U	E	M	A
R	W	L	X	R	A	A	W	S	L
U	E	L	I	T	E	I	D	Q	U
B	U	O	S	T	X	N	V	I	M
N	R	O	C	S	S	T	M	F	E
V	H	C	H	Z	W	A	Y	O	B
U	L	J	Z	A	V	N	H	W	D
D	R	M	L	M	G	C	S	I	H
P	S	L	U	M	B	E	R	T	P
N	O	I	C	I	P	S	U	S	Y
W	N	G	X	K	Q	J	N	Y	K
Y	J	Q	C	Y	R	W	A	Q	G

smug
amble
scorn
admire
wallow
hastily
slumber
shrewd
emulate
suspicion
acquaintance

Vocabulary Review Crossword I

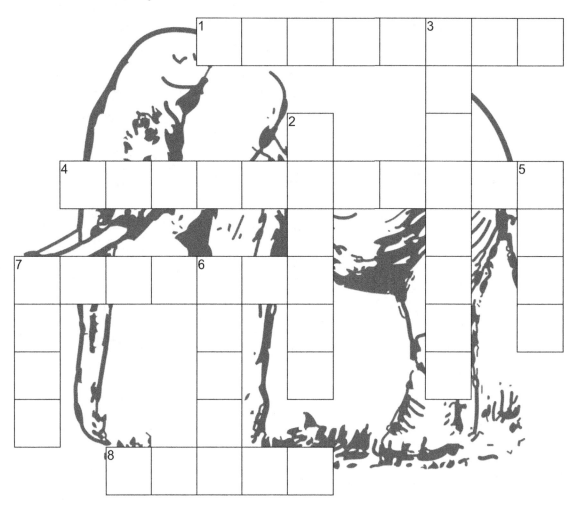

Across
1. knock down a building
4. thinking only of yourself
7. imitate someone to try to achieve what they have
8. shine brightly

Down
2. clever
3. with great focus, with eager attention
5. having too much pride in yourself
6. walking in a slow, relaxed way
7. jealous

Vocabulary Review Crossword II

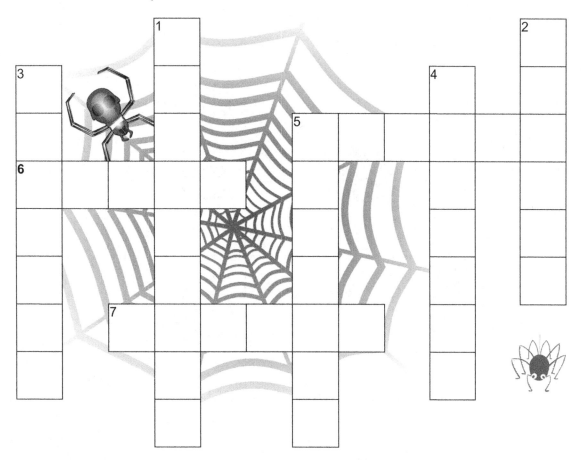

Across

5. to have a good opinion of something, to respect someone
6. thinking that someone or something is worthless or despicable
7. lie relaxed in mud or water

Down

1. poor condition of a building because no one is caring for it
2. lacking physical strength
3. doing something in a hurry
4. having honor and respect
5. worried

Vocabulary Review Crossword III

Across
1. unfair
5. swelling or protruding
6. someone you know, but not really well

Down
2. happy and at ease
3. feeling angered or annoyed
4. not showing respect to someone who deserves respect

BETTER BY FAR YOU SHOULD FORGET AND SMILE THAN THAT YOU SHOULD REMEMBER AND BE SAD. — CHRISTINA ROSSETTI

Vocabulary Review Word Jumble I

Unscramble the jumbled words to find a hidden word.

doing something in a hurry

L Y I H S T A

not showing respect to someone who deserves respect

P U M E I N D T

thinking that someone or something is worthless or despicable

C N R S O

imitate someone to try to achieve what they have

A L U E E T M

knock down a building

I H O L E S D M

Staying up too late makes me ◯ ◯ ◯ ◯ ◯ !

Vocabulary Review Word Jumble II

Unscramble the jumbled words.

a feeling or belief that someone is guilty

S O U C I N S I P   ➜ _____

thinking that someone or something is worthless or despicable

O C N R S   ➜ _____

to have a good opinion of something, to respect someone

M R I D E A   ➜ _____

not showing respect to someone who deserves respect

D T P U N E I M   ➜ _____

imitate someone to try to achieve what they have

T L M U E A E   ➜ _____

someone you know, but not very well

U I Q A N E C A N C A T   ➜ _____

selfish, thinking only of yourself

O L U G T T S H S E H   ➜ _____

having too much pride in yourself

U S G M   ➜ _____

Vocabulary Review Word Jumble III

Unscramble the jumbled words.

walking in a slow, relaxed way

L B A E M   → _____

lacking physical strength

E E B E F L   → _____

lie relaxed in mud or water

W L A O W L   → _____

doing something in a hurry

T S Y H L I A   → _____

feeling angered or annoyed

N A I N T I N G D   → _____

having honor and respect

I I N D G T Y   → _____

knock down a building

S E I D H M L O   → _____

with great focus, with eager attention

T N L Y T E I N   → _____

Vocabulary Review Word Jumble IV

Unscramble the jumbled words.

frustrated, very irritated

E T A X D S R P E E A → _____

poor condition of a building because no one is caring for it

I S D I R R E P A → _____

shine brightly

G A M L E → _____

swelling or protruding

L B U E G → _____

jealous

V N Y E → _____

with endless energy, working without getting tired

T S Y L E R I L E S → _____

worried

N S I U X O A → _____

clever

W S D R H E → _____

Vocabulary Review Fill-in-the-Blanks I

Fill in the blanks to complete the sentences. Change the word forms if necessary.

scorn   thoughtless   impudent   FEEBLE   ADMIRE

exasperated   bulge   ACQUAINTANCE   gleam   slumber

1. The moonlight _____ on the water.

2. Her grandfather is too _____ to work.

3. Her pockets were _____ with presents.

4. I was _____ by his endless grumbling.

5. She fell into a deep and peaceful _____.

6. He is not a friend, only an _____.

7. I really _____ your enthusiasm.

8. How could you be so _____?

9. She _____ their views as old-fashioned.

10. His _____ remark made them angry.

Vocabulary Review Fill-in-the-Blanks II

Fill in the blanks to complete the sentences. Change the word forms if necessary.

hastily   disrepair   **DEMOLISH**   contented

suspicion   shrewd   dignity   emulate

1. The _____ man devised a secret plan.

2. The factory is due to be _____ next year.

3. She accepted the criticism with quiet _____.

4. He was arrested on _____ of being a spy.

5. Classical music made them _____ and restful.

6. The building has fallen into _____ over the years.

7. The boy tried to _____ the famous baseball player.

8. I hastily _____ my homework before the game started.

Vocabulary Review Fill-in-the-Blanks III

Fill in the blanks to complete the sentences. Change the word forms if necessary.

intently	envy	anxious	tirelessly
wallow	indignant	amble	injustice

1. She _____ looked into my eyes.

2. Parents are naturally _____ for their children.

3. He was very _____ at the way he had been treated.

4. She was full of _____ when her sister won the contest.

5. We work _____ to ensure the streets are safe and clean.

6. We like to _____ through the park on Saturdays.

7. The boy who cheated won the game. What an _____!

8. Pigs do not sweat, so they _____ in mud to cool their bodies.

Synonyms Matching I

Synonyms are words that have the same or nearly the same meaning. Can you match the words with their synonyms? (The solution is on page 73.)

angry	assist
below	purchase
buy	awful
close	mad
help	choose
mix	annoy
business	under
bad	combine
pick	shut
bother	company

Synonyms Matching II

Synonyms are words that have the same or nearly the same meaning. Can you match the words with their synonyms? (The solution is on page 73.)

information ●	● sofa
part ●	● conclusion
find ●	● soil
equal ●	● component
ending ●	● conflict
get ●	● data
couch ●	● same
dirt ●	● locate
picture ●	● receive
fight ●	● image

Synonyms Matching III

Synonyms are words that have the same or nearly the same meaning. Can you match the words with their synonyms? (The solution is on page 73.)

throw	keep
cry	wish
filthy	middle
damp	toss
lid	greedy
save	dirty
fire	sob
hope	cover
selfish	wet
center	flame

Synonyms Matching IV

Synonyms are words with similar meanings. Write a synonym for each word.
Use the words from the word box. (The solution is on page 73.)

JOB   inspect   trousers   little   royal

eNd   PRAISE   over   street   earth

compliment	
above	
finish	
small	
examine	
pants	
road	
faithful	
work	
world	

Synonyms Matching V

Write a synonym for each underlined word. Use the words from the word box.
(The solution is on page 74.)

Mad   QUICKLY   tidy   shut   dirty

speak   RIGHt   start   AWFUL   glad

Let's <u>begin</u> the lesson. _____

Your answer is <u>correct</u>. _____

I need to <u>talk</u> with you. _____

I'm <u>happy</u> to see you. _____

Are you <u>angry</u> with me? _____

Please <u>close</u> the door. _____

I ran as <u>fast</u> as possible. _____

The smell is <u>terrible</u>. _____

The room is <u>messy</u>. _____

Your room is very <u>neat</u>. _____

Antonyms Matching I

Antonyms are words that have opposite or nearly opposite meanings. Can you match the words with their antonyms? (The solution is on page 74.)

more •	• add
forward •	• female
loose •	• straight
part •	• backward
subtract •	• less
male •	• whole
harm •	• tight
visible •	• sunny
bent •	• benefit
cloudy •	• invisible

Antonyms Matching II

Antonyms are words that have opposite or nearly opposite meanings. Can you match the words with their antonyms? (The solution is on page 74.)

fall	different
increase	solution
problem	divide
multiply	rise
positive	complex
hire	decrease
similar	negative
follow	rare
simple	lead
common	fire

Antonyms Matching III

Antonyms are words with opposite or nearly opposite meanings. Can you match the words with their antonyms? (The solution is on page 74.)

tall	bland
proud	found
strange	sweet
absent	short
colorful	refuse
against	normal
bitter	ashamed
lost	for
borrow	present
accept	lend

Antonyms Matching IV

Antonyms are words with opposite meanings. Write an antonym for each word. Use the words from the word box. (The solution is on page 74.)

create   dULL   win   exit   buy

top   IGNORE   quiet   LONG   unprepared

enter	
prepared	
destroy	
loud	
listen	
lose	
short	
shiny	
bottom	
sell	

Antonyms Matching V

Write an antonym for each underlined word. Use the words from the word box.
(The solution is on page 74.)

SLOWLY   WET   BACKWARD   stop   first
west   cold   right   COMPLICATED   cloudy

Let's go to the left.

It's hot today.

The sun rises in the east.

My clothes are dry.

I ran as fast as possible.

This is the last chapter.

The car moved forward.

The question is simple.

The weather is sunny.

Let's begin the lesson.

Synonyms or Antonyms?

Synonyms are words with similar meanings, and antonyms are words with opposite meanings. Tell whether each pair of words are synonyms or antonyms. (The solution is on page 75.)

Word Pairs	Which?
top, bottom	
happy, delighted	
sorrowful, sad	
answer, solution	
calm, windy	
sink, float	
cold, freezing	
tired, exhausted	
full, empty	
far, close	

Homophones Fill-in-the-Blanks I

Homophones are words that sound the same but have different meanings and spellings. Choose the correct homophone for each sentence. (The solution is on page 75.)

ate *or* eight?

I got up at _____ o'clock.

cell *or* sell?

A biologist studies _____ activities.

flour *or* flower?

Cake and cookies are made of _____.

one *or* won?

My team _____ the game yesterday.

sea *or* see?

The blue whale is the biggest _____ mammal.

Homophones Fill-in-the-Blanks II

Homophones are words that sound the same but have different meanings and spellings. Choose the correct homophone for each sentence. (The solution is on page 75.)

---

their *or* **there?**

They lost _____ toys somewhere over _____.

---

air *or* **heir?**

Humans cannot live without _____.

---

allowed *or* **aloud?**

You are not _____ to run in the halls.

---

ant *or* **aunt?**

My mom's sister is my _____.

---

ark *or* **arc?**

Noah took two of each animal on his _____.

Homophones Fill-in-the-Blanks III

Homophones are words that sound the same but have different meanings and spellings. Choose the correct homophone for each sentence. (The solution is on page 75.)

piece *or* peace?

Would you like to have a _____ of pie?

whole *or* hole?

He dug a deep _____ with his spade.

deer *or* dear?

_____ feed on a grass, twigs, and bark.

blue *or* blew?

She made a wish and _____ the candles out.

bury *or* berry?

She picked a _____ from the bush.

Homophones Fill-in-the-Blanks IV

Homophones are words that sound the same but have different meanings and spellings. Choose the correct homophone for each sentence. (The solution is on page 75.)

tail *or* tale?

The dog is wagging his _____.

by *or* buy?

I arrived at the airport _____ train.

tea or tee?

Would you like a cup of _____?

here *or* hear?

Can you _____ the noise outside?

weak *or* week?

He was too _____ to stand.

Prefixes & Suffixes I

A prefix is a word part placed in front of a root word. Add a prefix to each word. (The solution is on page 75.)

re	in/im	mis	un	dis

_____use

_____place

_____happy

_____take

_____play

_____agree

_____like

_____possible

_____comfortable

_____capable

_____cover

_____view

_____appear

_____lucky

_____zip

_____clear

_____polite

_____honest

_____able

_____match

Prefixes & Suffixes II

A suffix is a word part placed at the end of a root word. Add a suffix to each word. (The solution is on page 76.)

able	ful	al	ion	y

predict_____   success_____

comfort_____   logic_____

construct_____   reason_____

luck_____   peace_____

help_____   health_____

notice_____   joy_____

subtract_____   wonder_____

thank_____   touch_____

gloom_____   agree_____

care_____   predict_____

Prefixes & Suffixes III

A prefix is a word part placed in front of a root word, and a suffix is a word part placed at the end of a root word. Match the words with their definitions. (The solution is on page 76.)

slower	unable	fearless	joyful	biggest
untidy	worthless	careful	unhappy	disagree

_____ = the most big

_____ = with no worth

_____ = not happy

_____ = without fear

_____ = full of joy

_____ = not clean

_____ = more slow

_____ = you can't do it

_____ = not agree

_____ = with care

World Currencies Word Search

Find the countries and their currencies. The words can go in any direction, even backwards! (The solution is on page 76.)

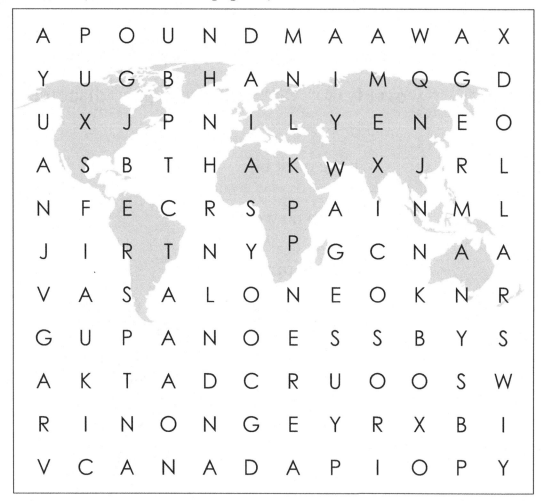

```
A  P  O  U  N  D  M  A  A  W  A  X
Y  U  G  B  H  A  N  I  M  Q  G  D
U  X  J  P  N  I  L  Y  E  N  E  O
A  S  B  T  H  A  K  W  X  J  R  L
N  F  E  C  R  S  P  A  I  N  M  L
J  I  R  T  N  Y  P  G  C  N  A  A
V  A  S  A  L  O  N  E  O  K  N  R
G  U  P  A  N  O  E  S  S  B  Y  S
A  K  T  A  D  C  R  U  O  O  S  W
R  I  N  O  N  G  E  Y  R  X  B  I
V  C  A  N  A  D  A  P  I  O  P  Y
```

The United Kingdom uses the <u>Pound</u>.
<u>France</u>, <u>Germany</u>, <u>Italy</u>, and <u>Spain</u> use the <u>Euro</u>.
<u>China</u> uses the <u>Yuan</u>, and <u>Japan</u> uses the <u>Yen</u>.
<u>Mexico</u> uses the <u>Peso</u>, and <u>Vietnam</u> uses the <u>Dong</u>.
<u>Australia</u> and <u>Canada</u> use their own types of <u>Dollars</u>.

Solutions to Selected Activities

Page 11
Lily's Walk Word Search

The first letters are marked. Remember that the words can go in any direction!

Page 26
Vocabulary Review Word Search

The first letters are marked. Remember that the words can go in any direction!

Page 33
Old Mr. Toad Word Search

The first letters are marked. Remember that the words can go in any direction!

Page 38
Jimmy Skunk Word Search

The first letters are marked. Remember that the words can go in any direction!

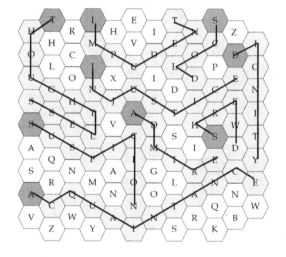

Page 41

Vocabulary Review Word Search

The first letters are marked. Remember that the words can go in any direction!

Page 52

Synonyms Matching I

angry – mad
below – under
buy – purchase
close – shut
help – assist
mix – combine
business – company
bad – awful
pick – choose
bother – annoy

Page 53

Synonyms Matching II

information – data
part – component
find – locate
equal – same
ending – conclusion
get – receive
couch – sofa
dirt – soil
picture – image
fight – conflict

Page 54

Synonyms Matching III

throw – toss
cry – sob
filthy – dirty
damp – wet
lid – cover
save – keep
fire – flame
hope – wish
selfish – greedy
center – middle

Page 55

Synonyms Matching IV

compliment – praise
above – over
finish – end
small – little
examine – inspect
pants – trousers
road – street
faithful – royal
work – job
world – earth

Page 56

Synonyms Matching V

begin – start
correct – right
talk – speak
happy – glad
angry – mad
close – shut
fast – quickly
terrible – awful
messy – dirty
neat – tidy

Page 57

Antonyms Matching I

more – less
forward – backward
loose – tight
part – whole
subtract – add
male – female
harm – benefit
visible – invisible
bent – straight
cloudy – sunny

Page 58

Antonyms Matching II

fall – rise
increase – decrease
problem – solution
multiply – divide
positive – negative
hire – fire
similar – different
follow – lead
simple – complex
common – rare

Page 59

Antonyms Matching III

tall – short
proud – ashamed
strange – normal
absent – present
colorful – bland
against – for
bitter – sweet
lost – found
borrow – lend
accept – refuse

Page 60

Antonyms Matching IV

enter – exit
prepared – unprepared
destroy – create
loud – quiet
listen – ignore
lose – win
short – long
shiny – dull
bottom – top
sell – buy

Page 61

Antonyms Matching V

left – right
hot – cold
east – west
dry – wet
fast – slowly
last – first
forward – backward
simple – complicated
sunny – cloudy
begin – stop

Page 62
Synonyms or Antonyms?

Synonyms
happy – delighted
sorrowful – sad
answer – solution
cold – freezing
tired – exhausted

Antonyms
top – bottom
calm – windy
sink – float
full – empty
far – close

Page 63
Homophones Fill-in-the-Blanks I

eight
cell
flour
won
sea

Page 64
Homophones Fill-in-the-Blanks II

their, there
air
allowed
aunt
ark

Page 65
Homophones Fill-in-the-Blanks III

piece
hole
deer
blew
berry

Page 66
Homophones Fill-in-the-Blanks IV

tail
by
tea
hear
weak

Page 67
Prefixes & Suffixes I

reuse, misuse	recover, uncover, discover
misplace	review
unhappy	disappear
mistake	unlucky
replay	unzip
disagree	unclear
unlike	impolite
impossible	dishonest
uncomfortable	unable, disable
incapable	rematch, mismatch

Page 68
Prefixes & Suffixes II

predictable	successful
comfortable	logical
construction	reasonable
lucky	peaceful
helpful	healthy
noticeable	joyful
subtraction	wonderful
thankful	touchable
gloomy	agreeable
careful	prediction

Page 69
Prefixes & Suffixes III

biggest
worthless
unhappy
fearless
joyful
untidy
slower
unable
disagree
careful

Page 70
World Currencies Word Search

The first letters are marked. Remember that the words can go in any direction!

Made in the USA
Monee, IL
14 May 2021